THE ROYAL YEAR 1989

PHOTOGRAPHED BY
TIM GRAHAM

MICHAEL O'MARA BOOKS LIMITED

88TH BIRTHDAY

4 August 1988

Queen Elizabeth the Queen Mother on her 88th birthday at Clarence House, her official residence in London. As is tradition on her birthday the Queen Mother came to the gates of Clarence House, accompanied by close members of her family including (right) the Queen and her granddaughter Lady Sarah Armstrong-Jones, to receive armfuls of bouquets from wellwishers.

On 5 August the Queen embarked on the Royal Yacht Britannia *at Southampton for the start of her annual cruise to the Western Isles of Scotland. As she was piped aboard, the ship's company of almost 300 stood to attention. Below: The Queen and her grandchildren, Zara and Peter Phillips, wave goodbye as the yacht prepares to leave Southampton.*

Overleaf: The Prince of Wales playing polo at Cirencester Park in Gloucestershire on 6 August. The Prince, one of Britain's top players, spends as many summer afternoons playing polo as his busy schedule permits.

ROYAL HOLIDAY
IN MAJORCA

August 1988

For the third year in succession the Spanish royal family were hosts to the Prince and Princess of Wales and their children for a short holiday in the sun at the Marivent Palace outside Palma on the Mediterranean island of Majorca.

Left: The Prince of Wales and Queen Sofia chat animatedly while posing for photographers on the steps of the Marivent Palace. Facing page: Prince William sitting with his cousin King Juan Carlos. Below: In Majorca the Prince and Princess of Wales enjoyed the chance to relax in the sun with their children, after a busy summer of official duties.

Facing page: It's back to school for Prince Henry after the long summer holidays and Prince William leaves his younger brother's nursery school wearing the mask he had made there during the morning. Left: On the following day, Prince Henry's birthday, term began for Prince William and the Princess of Wales and Prince Henry accompanied him back to Wetherby, his pre-prep school in Kensington. Below: Prince Henry leaving his nursery school on his birthday to return home to Kensington Palace.

THE YORKS IN AUSTRALIA

28 September – 7 October 1988

*The Duke of York, already in Australia
serving on his ship HMS* Edinburgh, *was
joined by his wife for their official visit to
the country as part of the bicentennial
celebrations. Below: On arrival at
Canberra airport at the start of the official
visit the Duke inspected the royal guard of
honour and band. Facing page: The official
duties during the Yorks' two-day visit
to the federal capital included a visit to
a child therapy centre.*

Above: The Duchess of York at the Chinese Gardens, Darling Harbour in New South Wales. Left: Meeting sailors of the Australian Navy at the Bicentennial Naval Review on 1 October in the spectacular setting of Sydney Harbour. The Duke of York was the Queen's Personal Representative and took the salute at the review along with the Prime Minister, Mr Bob Hawke. Right: The royal couple arriving for the dinner given that night by the Chief of Naval Staff.

This page: After church on Sunday 2 October the Duke and Duchess of York officially opened the Mount Annan Botanic Gardens at Kenny Hill outside Sydney. The gardens have been created to commemorate the bicentenary and for the occasion the Duchess of York wore a striking large green hat and floral dress. Facing page: The next day the royal couple travelled from Sydney north to Townsville in Queensland where they viewed an entertainment by young people at Queen's Park.

Facing page: At the Mount Gravett West Special School in Brisbane the Duke and Duchess of York saw work being done to help mentally and physically handicapped children. During the visit they chatted and played with children of all ages and overstayed their schedule by an hour. The Duchess confessed that she was missing her tiny baby, Princess Beatrice who was then only eight weeks old and far away back home in England. Right: The Duchess of York carrying out official engagements in Cloncurry, a remote outback area of North Queensland.

Left: Arriving at Parliament House in Brisbane for the State Reception given in their honour by the Governor of Queensland. Facing page: During a visit to the World Expo '88 exhibition in Brisbane on the last day of their busy tour the Duchess of York cuddled a koala bear named Bowie.

On 8 October Prince William was pageboy at the society wedding of Miss Camilla Dunne to the Hon. Rupert Soames, grandson of Sir Winston Churchill. Prince Henry was to have been a pageboy too but remained at home with a cold. Prince William looked very grown up in his ivory shirt, matching trousers and pink braces. The Prince and Princess of Wales, who was looking dazzling in aquamarine and black, attended the wedding along with 500 other guests.

THE QUEEN'S HISTORIC STATE VISIT TO SPAIN

17 – 21 October 1988

The Queen and the Duke of Edinburgh were warmly greeted by their cousins King Juan Carlos and Queen Sofia at the start of their five-day state visit to Spain, the first ever by a British reigning monarch. The Queen's royal hosts went to enormous trouble to make the visit an enjoyable and very successful one, accompanying them throughout their stay. Below: The first of many colourful moments of the visit was an inspection of the Spanish royal guard, dressed in their nineteenth-century style uniform, at the Pardo Palace in Madrid.

On the evening of their arrival the Queen and the Duke of Edinburgh were treated to a sumptuous state banquet at the Oriente Palace in Madrid. Left: The Queen greeting the Spanish royal children, Infanta Elena (left) and Infanta Cristina (right) and the Prince of the Asturias, heir to the Spanish throne. Below: The Queen, looking magnificent in Queen Mary's tiara and the Cambridge emeralds, posed with King Juan Carlos before dinner. The King is wearing his Garter badge as earlier in the day the Queen had appointed him an Extra Knight of the Garter, England's oldest and most noble order of chivalry. Facing page: Queen Sofia and the Duke of Edinburgh before the state banquet. Below: The two royal families assembled together.

Facing page: On the second evening of the visit the Queen gave a gala dinner at the Pardo Palace. For this occasion she wore a gold embroidered jacket and evening skirt with a necklace of diamonds and rubies. This page: Earlier in the day the Queen and the Duke of Edinburgh carried out engagements in Madrid.

Facing page: Thousands of people turned out to greet the royal party in Seville and after strolling around the historic city centre they watched a flamenco show in true Andalusian fashion in one of the courtyards of the Moorish Alcazar Palace. This page: The final day of the state visit was a trip to the Catalan city of Barcelona, including a visit to the site of the 1992 Olympic Games at Montjuich where they inspected a scale model of the stadium.

Over 800 people attended the Second Bruce Oldfield for Barnardo's Gala held at the Grosvenor House Hotel in London on 1 November. The Prince and Princess of Wales, President of Barnardo's, were guests of honour and as a compliment to her host, a former Barnardo's boy and now a leading fashion designer, the Princess wore a striking off-the-shoulder Bruce Oldfield dress of crushed velvet. At the gala evening which raised over £150,000 for Barnardo's, Bruce Oldfield (see right and below with the Princess) unveiled his spring and summer collections.

OFFICIAL VISIT TO FRANCE

7 – 11 November 1988

The Prince and Princess of Wales paid a triumphant five-day official visit to France during which the Prince was praised for his statesmanlike qualities and the Princess both for her care and compassion as well as for her beauty and excellent taste in clothes. This page: On arrival at Orly airport outside Paris the Princess delighted the awaiting French by wearing a Chanel outfit as a compliment to French haute couture. Facing page: At the official banquet at the Elysée Palace she wore a British-designed embroidered evening dress and bolero in shimmering white.

This page: The second day in Paris included a tour of the Musée d'Orsay (right and above left), a former railway station which now houses a magnificent museum of French art and sculpture, and a reception at the Hôtel de Ville (above right) given in their honour by Jacques Chirac, the Mayor of Paris. Facing page: The Princess of Wales at the British School of Paris at Croissy outside Paris.

Facing page: During their French stay the Prince and Princess of Wales went to the Loire Valley and visited the world-famous château of Chenonceau in its unique and picturesque position astride the river Cher. This page: For the romantic candlelit dinner at the château of Chambord which rounded off the stay in the Loire Valley the Princess wore a dazzling white and blue sequinned dress.

On the fourth day of their French visit the Prince and Princess of Wales went 'shopping' at Marks and Spencer, the British store over which even the chic Parisians rave. The branch in Paris was Marks and Spencer's first European store and is now one of their largest branches in the world.

For the dinner and reception given in the royal couple's honour by the British Ambassador the Princess wore a stylish, dramatic black and red evening dress designed by the French-born Catherine Walker of the Chelsea Design Company in London.

The final day in Paris saw a
solemn end to a triumphal visit.
It was 11 November, Armistice
Day, and the Prince and
Princess of Wales attended the
Arc de Triomphe Armistice
Commemoration followed by
the British Legion Ceremony
at Notre Dame Cathedral.
With President Mitterand at his
side, the Prince of Wales,
wearing the uniform of a colonel
of the Welsh Guards, laid a
wreath at the Arc de Triomphe
to remember the dead of two
world wars.

On 13 November, Remembrance Day, the Queen (below right) led the annual service of commemoration at the Cenotaph in Whitehall, London in honour of the nation's war victims and survivors. Watching from the Foreign Office balconies above Whitehall were (left) the Princess of Wales, Prince Edward, the Duchess of York, the Queen Mother and the Princess Royal; and (right) the Duchess of Kent, Lady Susan Hussey, lady-in-waiting to the Queen, the Duke and Duchess of Gloucester and Princess Alice, Duchess of Gloucester.

Facing page: The Prince of Wales spent the afternoon of his 40th birthday in Birmingham at a special party organized in his honour by the Prince's Trust, his own organization which helps young people to develop their business ideas. Over 1500 young people who had been helped by the Trust gathered at the Old Tram Depot in Aston to meet the Prince who was in excellent spirits. There was a magnificent birthday cake showing scenes of his life, including St Paul's Cathedral where he had married Lady Diana Spencer in 1981, and he enthusiastically joined in the dancing. After speeches and cake-cutting the Prince left to return to Kensington Palace in time for a family tea party with his children.

Right: On 18 November the Duchess of York attended a fundraising lunch at the Waldorf Hotel as a guest of the Jamaican High Commissioner to help in the island's rehabilitation after the devastating hurricane earlier in the year.

Whenever there is a new session of Parliament the Queen drives in State to Westminster for the State Opening of Parliament. It is an occasion of great pageantry and historic meaning and this year took place on 22 November. Below: Accompanied by a Sovereign's Escort of the Household Cavalry, the Queen drove to Westminster in the new Australian Coach, a bicentennial present from Australia. Far below: The Imperial State Crown travels to Westminster in advance of the Queen who then puts it on together with her Royal Robes in the Robing Room at the Palace of Westminster before proceeding through the Royal Gallery to the House of Lords.

Above left: The Duchess of York leaving the Barbican Centre on 21 November after attending the Polytechnic of Central London's Graduation Ceremony. Above right: The Princess of Wales in striking pink and black when she visited the Barnet Relate Centre at Tally-ho Corner, Finchley in north London.

Facing page: Wrapped up against the wintry weather in a warm coat and boots, the Princess of Wales visited Cowes on the Isle of Wight on 6 December as part of the war against drug smuggling. She performed the naming ceremony of the new Customs and Excise cutter Vigilant, *built to track down smugglers, at the FBM Marine shipyard and later went for a trip on board the* Vigilant *in the choppy waters of the Solent. Right: Prince Henry dressed as a shepherd boy on his way to his nursery school's nativity play on 8 December.*

Left: The Duchess of Kent, Patron of the Not-Forgotten Association, pouring tea for disabled and wounded servicemen and women at the organization's annual Christmas tea party held in the mews of Buckingham Palace on 9 December. Below and facing page above left: Prince and Princess Michael of Kent went to Sadler's Wells on 13 December to watch the ballet 'Snow Queen' in aid of the company's development appeal. Facing page above right: Prince Henry and the Princess of Wales arriving at the Palace Theatre in the West End of London on 13 December for Prince William's school Christmas concert. Below: On 19 December Princess Michael of Kent took her children, Lady Gabriella and Lord Frederick Windsor for a charity performance of 'Cinderella' at the Dominion Theatre in London's West End. After the show the royal party met members of the cast.

The christening of Princess Beatrice of York took place on 20 December at the Chapel Royal in St James's Palace. Left: The proud parents, the Duke and Duchess of York with their four-month old daughter. Below: The tiny princess in the royal christening robes of Honiton lace. Far below: The Prince and Princess of Wales with their children.

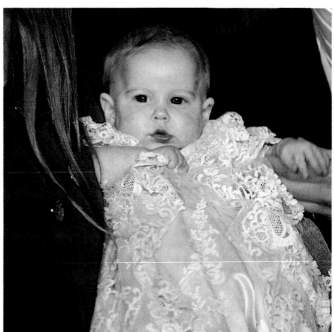

Because of major renovation work being carried out at Windsor Castle, in recent years the scene of the royal family's large Christmas gathering, Christmas was spent once again at Sandringham House, the Queen's private home in West Norfolk. Leaving church after the morning service on Christmas Day are (facing page above left) Captain Mark Phillips with his daughter Zara and Prince William; (facing page above right) the Duchess of Kent with her daughter Lady Helen Windsor; and (below) the Queen Mother talking to wellwishers with the Duchess of York and the Princess of Wales. Right: The Duchess of York and the Princess of Wales make a striking pair as they leave church to return to Sandringham House on foot.

THE PRINCESS OF WALES VISITS NEW YORK

1 – 3 February 1989

For her first official trip abroad alone the Princess of Wales went to New York for an action-packed three days. In her brief visit to this city of contrasts she saw some of the poorest areas of the city as well as the brash glitzy side for which New York is so famous. Thousands of people waited for hours in the cold to catch a glimpse of the Princess New Yorkers had been talking about for weeks. She lived up to their expectations in every way – glamorous and elegant as well as caring and compassionate.

Facing page left: A full day of engagements in Manhattan included visiting a day care centre, the Henry Street Centre on Lower East Side, one of the city's poorest areas. Facing page right: Shortly after her arrival from London on Concorde the Princess was guest of honour at a reception wearing a dazzling ruched blue top and black skirt with pearls and diamond earrings. Left: The Princess of Wales, Patron of the Welsh National Opera, arriving at their gala production of Falstaff at the Brooklyn Academy of Music. Below: On the final morning of the visit the Princess went to the Harlem Hospital Center to visit children suffering from Aids. The staff later had nothing but praise for her comforting words and the caring interest she had shown.

Left: On her return from New York the Princess of Wales was as busy as ever. On 8 February she went to Marston, Oxford to carry out two engagements, travelling in a helicopter of the Queen's Flight. Facing page above: The Princess of Wales chatting to ten-year-old Hitty, confined to a wheelchair, at the annual 'Mad Hatters Christmas Party' run by The London Taxidrivers' Fund for Underpriveleged Children at the Grosvenor House, Park Lane. Nearly 700 handicapped and underpriveleged children attended the teaparty.

Facing page: Evening engagements in town on 9 February. Right: The Duchess of York arriving at the Guildhall in the City of London for the Sports Aid Foundation Dinner. Far right: The Duchess of Gloucester was present at the Homeless Ball in aid of 'Homes for the Homeless' charity at the Hilton Hotel.

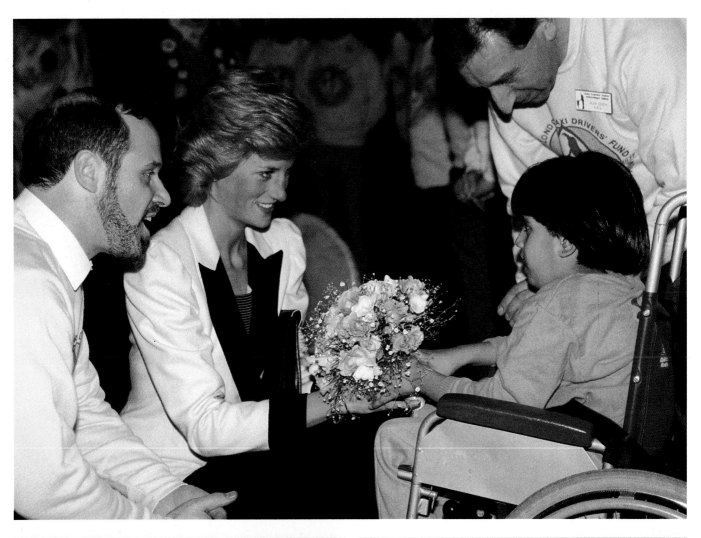

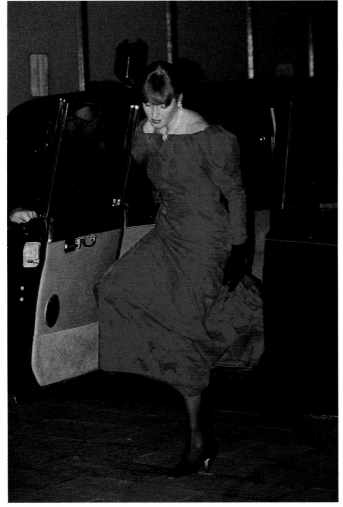

*Facing page: The Princess of
Wales visited Winchester
Cathedral on 2 March to attend
a Service of Dedication by the
1st Battalion The Royal
Hampshire Regiment of which
she is Colonel-in-Chief. The
service was followed by a
luncheon at Abbey House.
Wearing a striking red jacket
and hat designed by Arabella
Pollen, the Princess also wore
the regimental brooch presented
to her in 1985.*

*The Prince of Wales was back in
Klosters, Switzerland at the end
of February for a short skiing
holiday. It was a low-key affair
this year, following last year's
avalanche disaster and tragic
loss of life.*

Early March was a busy time for the royal ladies who were out and about at many different evening engagements. This page: Wearing a striking off-the-shoulder black velvet evening dress, the Princess of Wales went to the première of Dangerous Liaisons in aid of the Aids Crisis Trust on 6 March. Facing page left above: On 1 March the Duchess of York went to the première of Return from the River Kwai in aid of the Royal Academy of Arts. Left below: The Queen Mother at the Royal College of Music on 8 March for a Soirée d'Or recital. Right: The Princess of Wales went with Prince Charles on 9 March to the Savoy Centenary Ball in aid of Birthright, the mother/baby research charity of which she is Patron.

Left and facing page above: MacIntyre is a charity which runs homes for mentally handicapped adults and children. On 7 March the Duchess of York visited their administrative offices in Leighton Buzzard, Bedfordshire and talked to the waiting crowds. She then went on to visit two of their nearby homes.

Facing page below: The Queen Mother at the Royal Caledonian Schools in Bushey, Hertfordshire on 7 March to dedicate 'The Hall of Regiments'. The school is for children of officers and men of Scottish regiments and the Queen Mother has been one of the school's two Patrons since 1937.

AN OFFICIAL VISIT TO THE GULF

12 – 17 March 1989

In early March the Prince and Princess of Wales made a triumphant five-day visit to Kuwait and the United Arab Emirates. Despite the baking desert heat and the intricate Islamic customs such as strict dress codes which have to be observed, royal trips to the Middle East are always full of colour and interest. Right: The Princess in elegant blue and white silk stripes on arrival at Kuwait airport. Below: The formal audience with the Amir of Kuwait. Facing page: The Princess of Wales in stunning lilac silk with the Crown Prince at the Sha'ab Palace banquet.

This page: The climax of the Prince and Princess of Wales's visit to Kuwait was a morning spent at the Kuwait Museum of Islamic Art. Seated on silk cushions under a canvas awning they were served snacks of Arab sweetmeats and dates by girls dressed in colourful Bedouin costume. Facing page: For the last morning in Kuwait the Princess wore a striking dress in red and pink with gold trimmings. The strict Islamic dress codes require that hair, shoulders and knees should be covered in public.

The visit to Abu Dhabi included a picnic lunch in a desert oasis near Al Ain. The Prince and Princess of Wales thoroughly enjoyed the occasion – the many delicacies spread before them at this Bedouin feast included two whole roast sheep.

This page: Watching camel racing at Al Ain in Abu Dhabi. This exciting sport is very popular in the Middle East and the royal couple watched two races, enjoying the sight of the camel jockeys, small boys, perched precariously on top of the camels.

Facing page: For Dubai, the final stage of the Middle Eastern tour, the Princess wore a tailored jacket and skirt in blue and white with an enormous matching hat and turban.

This page: Only four days after the removal of her wisdom teeth the Princess of Wales was all smiles as she arrived for lunch at Claridge's, Mayfair on 4 April. She was there as Patron of Help the Aged to meet members of the charity's new industry and commerce committee. Facing page: The Duchess of York at Aintree Racecourse, Liverpool on 8 April for the 150th Grand National race.

THE GORBACHEVS MEET THE QUEEN AT WINDSOR

7 April 1989

It was a momentous moment in Anglo-Soviet relations when the Queen welcomed President and Mrs Gorbachev to Windsor Castle on the last day of their short stay in Britain. Accompanied by the Prime Minister and her husband, the Gorbachevs thoroughly enjoyed their visit to Windsor Castle, the largest privately inhabited castle in the world. After a brief welcoming ceremony nearly marred by April drizzle the Queen led her guests through the magnificent State Apartments to lunch in the State Dining-Room.

Facing page: The Gorbachevs drive through the Home Park and are received in a colourful welcoming ceremony by the Queen and the Duke of Edinburgh at the State Entrance. The 1st Battalion Coldstream Guards mounted a Guard of Honour in full ceremonial day dress in the centre of the Quadrangle. Left: Mrs Raisa Gorbachev with the Queen and Prince Edward, who was to visit Moscow the following week. Below: Before going inside the castle President Gorbachev, accompanied by the Duke of Edinburgh, inspected the Guard of Honour.

Facing page above: On 20 April the Queen and the Duke of Edinburgh visited West and Mid-Glamorgan in Wales. After a drive through the Ogmore and Rhondda Valleys they stopped in Treherbert, a small mining town. The following day the Queen spent her birthday at magnificent Powis Castle, near Welshpool in Powys where, as Colonel-in-Chief of the Royal Welch Fusiliers, she took part in the regiment's tercentenary celebrations. Facing page below: Being presented with a giant birthday cake which she then helped to cut. Right: The colourful pageant illustrating the history of the regiment included American soldiers dressed in uniform worn at the time of the American War of Independance.

Below: On 25 April the Queen Mother, Colonel-in-Chief of the Light Infantry, spent a full day at the Light Division Depot, Sir John Moore Barracks, Winchester in Hampshire. Here she is chatting to soldiers in camouflage who had just taken part in the military pageant depicting life at the Depot.

Facing page: The Princess of Wales enjoying herself at the national launch of 'Bike '89' in Hyde Park on 18 April. The launch was in aid of the British Lung Foundation whose Patron is the Princess. 'Bike '89' organized by the Cyclists Touring Club aims to promote cycling as a healthy, enjoyable pastime but the Princess politely declined to get on a bike and cycle round the Park, joking that her skirt was too tight. Right: However, she donned a more sporty look when she took Prince Henry to his nursery school at the start of his summer term on 25 April.

Above left: The Duchess of
Gloucester at the Enham Village
Settlement, Hampshire on
27 April where, as Patron of the
Papworth and Enham
Foundation, she turned the first
turf of a £1 million resource
centre for disabled people.
Above right: The Queen
inspecting a pigsty at the British
Food and Farming Exhibition in
Hyde Park on 5 May which she
had just opened.

Left: The Prince of Wales
standing on the Kop, the famous
terraces at the Anfield football
ground in Liverpool. During a
day of official engagements in
Liverpool on 3 May the Prince
took time to visit Anfield to pay
tribute to the dead and injured
after the recent Hillsborough
disaster.

At Beccles Heliport on 26 April the Duchess of York is ready to leave by helicopter for her visit to the Shell/Esso Leman Alpha Gas platform off the East Anglian coast. The Duchess joked to onlookers that it was difficult to look good in her orange survival suit.

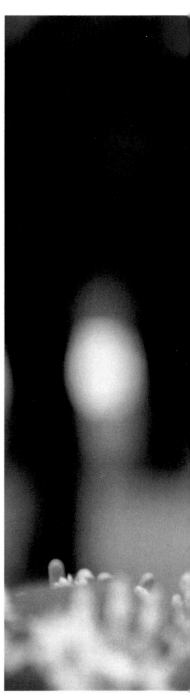

*The Queen at the Royal
Windsor Horse Show on
13 May when she watched
Prince Philip compete in the
marathon stage of the
International Driving Grand
Prix. Prince Philip, one of
Britain's top three-day event
competitors, was driving the
Queen's team of fell ponies.*

On 14 May the Princess of
Wales took the salute at the
Combined Cavalry 'Old
Comrades' Annual Parade and
Memorial Service in Hyde Park.

The Duchess of Kent, Patron of the International Social Service of Great Britain, at the 30th Spring Fair on 17 May at Kensington Town Hall. The Duchess was joined by diplomats' children dressed in their national costumes to help cut the 30th anniversary cake baked by the Mayor of Kensington.

Two major naval events took the Queen to Portsmouth, Hampshire on 18 May. Right: In the morning she visited HMS Dolphin at Gosport and presented a new Colour to Submarine Command. She is seen here taking the salute on the parade ground. Below and facing page: In the afternoon the Queen attended the Re-Commissioning Ceremony of the carrier, HMS Invincible. Having toured the ship she then met members of the ship's company and their families.

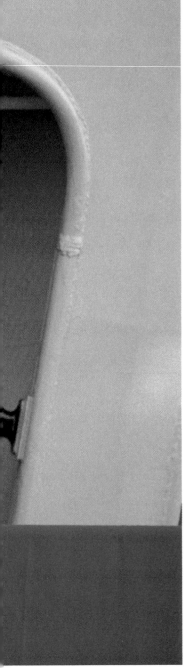

Left: The Prince of Wales with Major Ronald Ferguson, his polo manager, on 7 May at Cirencester Park Polo Club. The Prince was playing his first match of the 1989 season. Facing page: On 22 May the Duchess of York, Patron of the Dulwich Picture Gallery, visited the gallery in south London to attend a teaching session for disabled children. She happily lent a helping hand, much to the delight of eight-year-old Sonia Hakin.

THE DUCHESS OF YORK VISITS WEST BERLIN

24 – 26 May 1989

For the first time the Duchess of York travelled abroad to represent the Queen. She went to West Berlin for the Queen's Birthday Parade on 26 May. Her growing confidence and poise were evident and she carried out her engagements with great success. Below: After her arrival at RAF Gatow, the Duchess inspected the Guard of Honour. Right: In another striking black and white outfit the Duchess took the royal salute at the Queen's Birthday Parade at the Maifeld Olympic Stadium and reviewed the parade of 1,000 soldiers.

During her visit the Duchess of York saw some of the city sights, including a view of the Berlin Wall and the Brandenburg Gate beyond in East Berlin.

Left: On 6 June the Princess of Wales, Patron of the Guinness Trust, went to Hackney in the East End of London to open the Trust's Lorne House Project for Drug and Alcohol Dependency. Below: The Princess of Wales arriving at the Royal Opera House on 7 June for a royal gala performance of Il Trovatore.

Left: The Queen with her private secretary, Sir William Heseltine, at the Derby on 7 June. Derby Day is always a favourite occasion with the Queen who is a keen racegoer and one of the largest thoroughbred owners in Britain.

Facing page and below: On 8 June the Prince and Princess of Wales visited Northampton where the Princess received the honorary Freedom of the Borough. Before the ceremony at the Guildhall there were other engagements in the town, including inspection of the guard of honour provided by officers and men of The Royal Pioneer Corps outside the Church of the Holy Sepulchre.

Facing Page: Trooping the Colour, the colourful ceremony to mark the sovereign's official birthday, took place this year on 17 June. The Queen Mother travelled from Buckingham Palace to Horse Guards Parade with the Princess of Wales and Princes William and Henry. This was the first year that Prince Henry attended the spectacular ceremony. Right: The Queen no longer rides sidesaddle at Trooping the Colour but travels in a small carriage. Below: After Trooping the Colour is over there is a flypast by the Royal Air Force and watching from the balcony of Buckingham Palace were (from left to right) the Duchess of Kent, Prince and Princess Michael of Kent with their two children, Lady Gabriella and Lord Frederick Windsor, Princess Margaret, the Princess of Wales with Princes William and Henry, the Prince of Wales, the Queen, Prince Philip, the Duke and Duchess of York, the Queen Mother and Lady Rose Windsor.

Facing page: The Queen in procession on her way to St George's Chapel on 19 June for the annual Garter Day Service. Garter Day is one of the oldest English traditions and takes place at Windsor Castle at the beginning of Royal Ascot Week. The Queen is head of the Order founded by Edward III in 1348 and walks in procession with the Knights of the Garter to St George's Chapel. Right: The King of Spain, installed as a new Knight at the Service, walks in procession with the Prince of Wales and the Queen Mother to St George's Chapel. Below: After the service the Queen Mother and Queen Sofia of Spain returned to Windsor Castle by carriage.

At Royal Ascot the royal party arrive from nearby Windsor Castle in open landaus before the start of each afternoon's racing and drive up the course to the Royal Enclosure to applause from the crowds. Left: The Prince of Wales and the Duke of Kent. Centre left: The Queen Mother and the Duchess of Kent with the Hon. Sir Angus Ogilvy seated opposite. Below left: The Duchess of York and Princess Margaret. Below: This year the Princess Royal brought along her eight-year-old daughter, Zara to watch the first day's racing at Royal Ascot, by special permission as children under twelve are not normally allowed in the Royal Enclosure.

Facing page: Walking through the crowds to and from the paddock at Royal Ascot were (left) Prince and Princess Michael of Kent, (right) the Duchess of York and (below) the Princess of Wales.

THE ROYAL YEAR · 111

On 29 June the Prince of Wales took his young sons to watch Beat the Retreat at the Orangery, Kensington Palace. Princess Margaret lives at Kensington Palace as does the Prince of Wales and his family and so she accompanied them on the short walk to the Orangery from the Palace. Overleaf: Prince William and Prince Henry at Beat the Retreat. Even young princes have to master the royal art of standing still.

A series of new official photographs of the Duke and Duchess of Gloucester taken by Tim Graham at their London home at Kensington Palace in the summer of 1989. In the formal photograph the Duke is wearing the insignia of the Grand Cross of the Royal Victorian Order, an honour which the Queen granted to the Duchess shortly afterwards.

Facing page: The Duke and Duchess of York arriving hand-in-hand for the farewell dinner at Charlottetown on Prince Edward Island during their second official visit to Canada in July. The Duchess was looking radiant in an embroidered evening gown by Hardy Amies and the diamond tiara was a wedding present from the Queen three years earlier. Left: On the third day on Prince Edward Island the Duchess of York wore a bright yellow jacket and black skirt to visit the Basin Head fisheries museum. Right: The Duke of York waving to the crowds during the successful visit to Canada. Below: The Duke and Duchess of York meeting a falcon, Miss Piggy at a Quebec nature reserve. On the tour the royal couple seemed overjoyed to have so much time together as they have to endure many weeks of separation each year because of the Duke's commitments with the Royal Navy.

Overleaf: On 23 July the Princess of Wales enjoyed a relaxing afternoon at polo with Prince William.

First published in Great Britain in 1989 by Michael O'Mara Books Limited,
9 Lion Yard, 11–13 Tremadoc Road, London SW4 7NF
in association with Independent Television News Limited

A CIP catalogue record for this book is available from the British Library

ISBN 0-948397-36-5

Designed by Martin Bristow
Edited by Fiona Holman

Typeset by Florencetype Ltd, Kewstoke, Avon
Printed and bound by Printer Industria Grafica SA, Barcelona, Spain